Our Little Book of Hope

Edited by
Beth Abbott

Copyright © 2021 Beth Abbott

ISBN: 9798510086720

PublishNation
www.publishnation.co.uk

Introduction

We wanted to create a little book of hope during a time where so many people felt lost.

We know that in years to come the days of Covid-19 will be written about in History books, so we thought we could all have a little keepsake of our very own.

I thought about some of the places that most need a little hope like doctor's surgeries, Rehabilitation centres, hospices and the people who live on the streets.

It's so easy when you are in a dark place to forget about the beauty in the world. So, I thought we could write about the things we are grateful for or the things in life we love.

This is to show that even in the darkest days there can be some light. There can be beauty found in a smile from a stranger, a walk in Nature or hopefully found inside the pages of our little book of hope.

We hope that you enjoy reading this and that if you have a hobby or passion, it encourages you to follow your dreams.

Every word written on paper and every stroke of the brush can help to release feelings that you have from within, so whether it be that you want to write it down and rip it up, or collect your work for your own book one day, its better out on the page than stuck inside your mind.

I hope that you enjoy this and I send love in the hope that your dark days get brighter my friend.

We would like to say a special thank you to Create Recovery for giving us the opportunity to make this book possible for paying for the publishing. I would also like to say a massive thank you to everyone who handed me their work to help with the creation of this book it truly warmed my heart.

www.createrecovery.org

If you read this book and would like to get involved in any future creative projects, please feel free to contact on www.btdtpoetryworkshops.com.

Hope

Hope is the place you want to go
Hope is the person you want to know
Hope is the feeling that carries you through
Hope is the future for me and you

Written by Maddie age 13

Hope

Hope is a world that keeps you alive
Hope is a word that gives you strength with all your
struggles and strives
Hope is a word that gives us life
Hope says hold on and the pain will end
So, hold on my friend
And things will be fine

Written by Tilly Mai Vanacore Age 11

Summer

Summer warm
Summer tan great
Sun burns no
Summer, Summer I need sun cream
Yes, yes or you burn

Written By Lilly Age 6

Volcano

Big Ashes in the sky
White grey clouds filling the sky
Red yellow orange magma seeping through the volcano
Far, far greedy grass wing through the sky
Rocks chipping slowly
Magma tears into, magma flooding on top of the lava

Written by Lilly Age 6

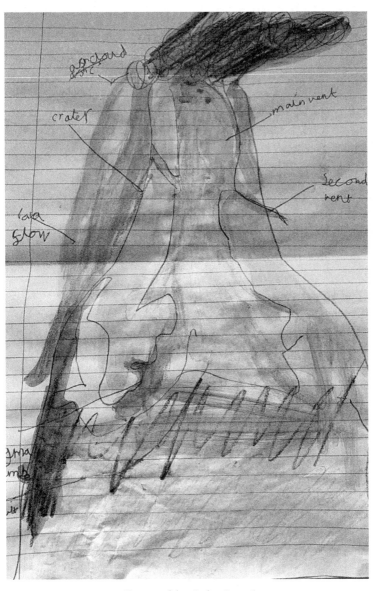

Created by Lily Age 6

What Covid is like through the eyes of a 6-year-old

Covid has made many people sick.
Covid is very bad.
It makes me mad and sad.
It's killed many sick people get it like dad and others.
Doctors and nurses also paramedics help a lot to keep you and me safe.
During Covid I have been at home playing with my brother and having lots of treats.
I even went to Bristol with six people in my family.
I even had my Birthday with lots of cards presents and money.

Written by Abbie age 6

What Covid is like through the eyes of a 4-year-old

Covid is bad because it can make people sick and can also make them died.
It made me sad and upset because you wouldn't like it if it was your family got sick and died.
People like Doctors and Nurses police are very good because they keep the world safe.

Written by Sam age 4

Created by Abbie age 6

Fur Babies

It all started on the 29th of July, my 15th Birthday Where I met my best friend and instantly fell in love. My Mom and I went round to her friend's house for a catch-up and her cat had given birth to 3 adorable kittens, I looked at one of them and instantly knew she was the one. She was white all over with ginger and black spots all over her body, a little patch on her nose and a very stripy tail. We knew she was the one.

After 8 long weeks of waiting for her to come home the day finally came, before picking her up we went to the shop to buy all the essentials such as a bed, food bowls, toys, food and of course a few treats for her then we drove to my mom's friend house and picked her up, we decided to call her Nala and it was so perfect for her. On the drive home she sat in my arms looking around wondering where we were taking her.

We finally got home and put her down on the floor letting her wonder, we put some food down for her in case she was hungry and then we played with her and her toys, she was so playful but after a while she got tired so she fell asleep in my arms for an hour or two, when she woke up, she had some food and went to the toilet it was hard to litter train her first but after a while she did it. The first night she slept in my bed with me and cuddled up to me all night, she woke up a few times for food and the toilet but other than that it was a perfect first night.

Days went on and she was already getting so much bigger, when she finally settled down, she would leave my side and explore the house, she became a lot more playful and a lot more adventurous, she started going outside in the garden and playing around with the garden furniture and chasing the butterfly's then before we knew it, she was going out exploring and staying out with her friends all night like a teenager.

I used to get very scared when she never came home on the nights but I'd wake up in the morning and she'd be down stairs on her favourite spot on the sofa catching up on all the sleep that she'd missed the night before.

Months and months past and she was nearly a 1-year-old kitten, one day we discovered that her belly was getting big very quickly and she wasn't acting herself, yep you guessed it she was pregnant! She was sleeping so so much and eating a lot more.

On the 25th of July it was my 16th Birthday party so I had invited friends and family round, as people started coming, I came upstairs to grab something and I heard a strange noise I checked on Nala and she was in labour!

There were already 2 kittens on the floor and I could see she was getting ready for the next one to arrive, I shouted my mom and Nan to come up stairs and there we were helping Nala give birth to kittens, people started arriving at my house wanting to see the kittens but it would've stressed Nala out so we told them to stay away.

Hours passed and her and her kittens were already so attached to each-other, they were constantly eating then sleeping and Nala was getting very tired from feeding them all the time so Nala was sleeping a lot of the time too.

Weeks were rapidly going by and the kittens were getting so much bigger so quickly, they started opening their eyes then before we knew it, they were running around the house fighting each other as they were getting old enough to not have to rely on their mom anymore, we had to start looking for homes for them.

Luckily, we kept one of them and the other two went to my Nan and my friend. I didn't want to let them go but I had to, I was happy I still got to see them all the time if I wanted to.

Firstly, one of the little boys went, my friend and her mom came over to pick him up, then a few days after we dropped Nalas only little baby girl off to my nans and then we were just left with one of them, which was the one we kept, he is black and white with stripes all over him. We named him Oreo, he was so perfect in every single way and we were so glad we decided to keep him.

He was growing up so fast, he and Nala are the best of friends, they fight a lot but that's what cats do. Oreo eventually started to explore the house on his own but Nala was always by his side at first protecting him.

After a few weeks Nala started to go outside again and leave Oreo to do his own thing, this meant we could get proper bonding time with Oreo without Nala having to worry, she wouldn't stay out for long though as she was still very protective of him.

Eventually Nala finally trusted us with him and started to stay out for hours again, coming back for food then going straight back out.

Oreo was growing up so fast, he was so playful but when we were tired, he was the cuddliest little kitten ever. He and Nala are best friends and I'm so glad they both have each-other to tell secrets to and to play together.

They are both my absolute world and there both my best friends. Everyone probably thinks I'm so silly but unless you have a fur baby, you'd never understand how special they are and the thought of losing them is the worst feeling in the world.

Nala and Oreo are both turning 1 and 2 in July; their birthdays are a day apart. They grow up so fast but I treasure every moment with them and love them with all my heart

Written by Amelia Truman Age 16

Our Cat Lynn

Our cat has big green eyes and a little pink nose
She has very long Whiskas and white tipped toes

She plays outside and climbs up trees
Jumping around chasing butterflies and bees

Then when she's ready she comes home to say
Meow feed me please I'm in to stay

Belly full and exhausted she falls asleep by the bin
We love our cat our cat called Lynn

Written by Donna Cash Age 50

Created by Alfie age 8

Created by Marie

13

Back To School

With Covid 19 we can't go to school
But going back is my number one rule
Now I'm back I feel great
Even enjoy my dinner on a big plate
I see my friends and we work and play
Let's hope Covid 19 will go away.

Written by Ava age 9

The feel of going back to school

Back Packs on
Moaning Mom
Lunch Ready
Easy and steady
Uniform Made
Don't Be afraid
Friends to see drink your tea
Teacher talking
Go to the school gates while walking
Playground play
You won't end the day
Chomp crunch
Munch, munch
Home times here
Go ahead and cheer.

Written by Isabella Martin age 9

Love The Most

Sundays
Used to be the worst days
Dealing with the aftermath of the weekend state
Now every Sunday there will always be a roast
upon our plate
There will be uniform clean and smelling fresh
No regrets of a weekend sesh
Just ordinary days forest walks,
Meaningful Mother daughter talks
Ordinary days without Drama are quite delightful
The beauty in soba sleep insightful
Rested, alert, aware
That it's still in me ingrained somewhere
So, I don't let it, even for a second, slip in my mind I
know its sneaky style
I don't walk by the Alcohol Isle
I have built up so much I truly love this peace
So, I Armour up to fight this beast
I take my dog for little walks on a Sunday
I actually embrace the thought of Monday
It doesn't send shivers down my spine
I polished the school shoes till they shine
It's just little things, not massive things
that normal people do
That you find joy in once again as your exploring
a fresh life new
It's not for brownie points or to gloat or Boast
I don't hate Sundays anymore, in fact I think
I love them the most

Written by Beth Abbott age 33

Carousel

Sometimes I want it all to disappear
or at least pretend it's not there
the paranoia... The anxiety...
Thinking that people just don't care
Waiting for that one text or call
The constant checking of the phone,
Hitting the bottle to drown it all out
And forever wanting to be alone
Carrying on with everyday life, despite all my fears
Every shower the water mingling with my tears
My mind like a carousel ride forever spinning round
Trying to block it out, every little sound
Taking happy pills to get through the day
I never thought I'd end up this way
Finding someone to talk to is the hardest thing of all
No one knows, no one understands...
Nobody seems to get my disaster of snowfall
All the visible scars but no visible pain
Just a person screaming inside trying to explain
The truth I learnt is it never goes away
Not unless you fight to want for another day
I'm strong, I'm humble and I've finally been found
It's not the load that breaks you down
It's the way you carry it around

Written by Scarlett Martin

Created by Vanessa

My Dyslexia and me

It's not easy having Dyslexia. It's a disability that no one can see.

I can't say I'm not proud to have it but it's certainly part of me.

"Why oh, why am I like this and why oh, why can't it belong to someone else." But I guess it's part of me and that is the way it's going to be.

I try to be organised but it's not part of my makeup I just live-in chaos because and there are times when I feel I just need a good shakeup.

But that is not the answer. It is those times when I know Dyslexia is surely part of me.

"I can't find this; I can't find that. Where're my glasses where have I put my keys and have you seen my phone?" These are the words I say several times a day.

Notwithstanding driving my car, I visit somewhere to come out of the road to go home and then can't remember which way to turn.

Do I tell people will think I'm stupid or will they just look and think thick!! But that is not the case. Because I'm wiser and think differently, I've been given a talent that no one else can see.

Now I know you're all reading this and thinking the same as me. No one is stupid, no one is thick. But I do wish this Dyslexia would leave me. It's not going to, is it?

I'm guessing I'm going to have to put up with it. I get names mixed up and if I give you that name when we first meet unfortunately it's stuck.

Sarah, Jane John Michael, Mohammed, Irsra what is your name. I cannot remember. I cannot dial telephone numbers the first-time. I get mixed up with my right and left or is that left and right. I guess I keep on trying to guess until I get it right?

But having said all of this. I have achieved many great things. I wrote this to help or even inspire others for you too may feel the same as me. Be assured that with a little help and understanding from others that you can put your mind to things and do anything you want to. We just learn differently to others. We think differently and have different ways of learning that others may never see. There is a magic that no one knows about and that's Dyslexia and me. One day I will have written my first book and I may take my own advice. "Believe in yourself and never let anyone tell you. "You can't do it" Because you can!! One last word or maybe two. Thank you for reading my poem as it was written to inspire you.

Written by Shirley

A Poem explaining what Been There Done That cic Does

I wanted to create an organisation that moved with the times
Tackling taboo subjects like Domestic Violence and County Lines
Hit hard and talk of the rehab centres at the end of substance abuse
Right to the front line and work with the youth
For my own teenage years is when the addiction got planted
I had not much knowledge of these things so I rebelled and gallivanted
So, I will be working in schools, showing where these paths can lead
Try to un sow the troublesome gateway weed
I want to talk about mental health and the impact of knife crime
Make them aware of places they can go to for help when life is not fine
Work together with other organisations and share the pots of money
I believe there is not just bear in the game so they don't need all the pots of honey
I want to empower the people I work with help them with their self-doubt

As if I was stepping back in time and empowering my teenage self
I want to talk about peer pressure and consequence
About a knife crime poem, I wrote of a mother talking of her son in the past tense
Talk about domestic violence and healthy relationships

How they can't say that they love but place fear in your heart with their fists
I want to talk of these subjects in a creative way
So, when they write their own words on paper, they are engrained they stay
I've done projects for places such as St Basils Charity
I lived in those hostels through consequence you see
I want to show in life it's your mind you have choices
Help the generation of tomorrow find their creative voices.

Written by Beth Abbott 33

Nature

The green dark
Misty by the park
The trees standing there
Animals looking for their prey beware
The River going fast
Never the last
The birds tweeting loud
Branches waving making a sound
The sun peeking through
I love it here, so should you

Written by Isabella Martin age 9

What is it that I do want?

Peace

So badly
So much
Just peace
Rest
Calm
Harmony
Warmth
Security
Safety

Peace
Love
Joy
Source

I can feel them now
In the evening
On my own

I look forward to having all these things
Truly
Present
Throughout The day

Written by Hannah de Quincey

The beauty of seeing my son's face light up
Intent on hearing my husband's whisper

Then Acting out planet earth
As a tight blob on the floor

Or mishearing run
And still guessed right
Or acting as a wall
By staying totally still
With Hands by his cheeks

His enthusiasm
And innocence
And creativity
And open joy
So
So
Beautiful
And transfixing

I wouldn't have missed this moment for the world

Written by Hannah de Quincey

The Law of Attraction...

First write it down for it to be received
Once words hit paper it can be believed
Focus on it everyday
Believe in your own words that you say
Negative mind-set can attract negative action
Like having a minus number then hitting it with
subtraction
For example, 'arr it's raining that's just my luck'
Mother Nature's not just out to get you she gives not one
fuck
If you have spent two hours straightening, your hair
She didn't go 'yes that house hers I'm going to rain right
there'
If you wake up with the mind-set you are going to be late
You have already got yourself worked up in a state
So, each traffic light it seems to stay on red
Till it's boiling piss right out your head
Change the mind set and calm the storm
Wake up 10 minutes earlier appreciate the dawn
Ground yourself with the day read the forecast
Let those anxious feeling just wizz right past
Don't store them up and let them bubble
For they will only lead you to trouble
Take one good thing out of each day
If it's a bad one better days are on the way
There is nothing bad about lessons learnt
Practice what you preach for dreams are earned
If you are feeling low or actually depressed
Practice if you can some mindfulness
Breathe all the way in slowly breathe out
Don't harbour in that fear and doubt...

Written By Beth Abbott

Gather 'Round, My Children

Many lifetimes ago,
In the time of Great Greed,
When chaos and shame were still dancing.
Division of truths, Harmony absent between them,
Sparked a moment of reckoning for all
The People were asleep at the wheel
They slumbered through war they sleepwalked through
pain,
They fought their invisible fights. "Wake, my people",
All whispered,
"Feed the Love that's within you, Remember the world
gifted, your Home".
But The People kept sleeping.
Lulled by their cravings,
Deceived by their wanting,
Within their borders never meant to be drawn
They argued and bickered,
Over lands and creators,
Voices shouting, unseen and unknown
But The People slept on.
From the earth came a message,
spread like fire among them,
Called for their courage and hearts to be One.
"Damage no more, Your Family is hurting,
Unity beckons, and the Time is right now"
And The People started to wake
More joined All in speaking,
Humanity's language,
the words that got lost on the way:
"We've forgotten our calling, to be keepers and makers,
Attend to this world and its kin".

The answers we long for, the key to survival Eternal, is
Love's Great Power within.
And so, My Dear Children,
The story was written
In perfect 2020 hindsight…
Dominion means Service,
What we have is not 'ours', misguided use of false power
did stop.
For The Virus was Love, Disguised, to remind us we're
creating together,
A journey of life… So, Wake up All People, to Love.

Written by Jodi from Canada

A Scottish Joke

I'll see you through the window,
Finished off a Scottish joke.
But now it's not so funny,
Cus to hug would make you choke
We have more weeks before we're free to live our lives
again
I pray we're safe and well by then and meet up for hugs ye
ken!

Written by Lynn

World War 3, the one we cannot see

Before the storm, we were eating more than just canned
corn
We were out in the pubs and bars, running errands in our
cars
Commuting on busy trains five times a week
To pay for the bills and for the life we all think we seek
And so, the invisible enemy came to play
Affecting schools, the NHS and our pay
But was this written in the stars before the very start
Showing that no country is different or apart
World War 3, the one we cannot see
It's showing us kindness and how to care
The importance of community and to share
Because who really needs to stockpile?
Or rush overflowing trolleys down the aisle
But the world has done so much for us
When all we do is pollute and use the bus
Nature even gave us toilet roll
Perhaps we can give back by limiting our stroll
To once a day so that Covid 19 won't stay.
World War 3, the one we cannot see
Has stopped our routines
Making us feel worried and eat extra greens
We have lost many lives
It's overtaking guns and knives
This we cannot do anything but send love
To all those affected and are now up above
And now we appreciate doctors and nurses like never
before
So, let's sit back, stay home and avoid the store
World War 3, the one we cannot see
But we will get through this as one

Until this invisible enemy is gone
Make laughter amongst the heaviness
Bake cakes, paint art and even get into fitness
Because for once the world is still
Letting us stay home, with family and simply chill
We have questioned when this will end
But then we paused, messaged a friend and pressed send
In all the chaos there were moments to reflect
Upon life, friends and family that we often neglect
And people were forced to think outside the box
To have fun wearing nothing but loungewear and big
socks
So maybe when the world returns
We will let go of silly fights and concerns
Because does it really matter
When you could speak only good words and flatter
You might go from bubble bath tubs
To drinking on the dance floors in the clubs
But just remember this feeling
Whilst you're still staring from wall to ceiling
World War 3,
The one we cannot see
From nowhere it came, things will never be the same

Written by Yasmin 29

(Must read in a Scottish accent)

To a virus, with apologies to The Bard Big sleeket ,
Horrible, infectious beastie,
Putting a panic in our breasties
I wish you'd run away sae hastie
Wi aw the speed that you can muster.
We're daen the best that we can do Self isolating,
Staying at hame,
It really is a crying shame
Daen puzzles just to keep us sane
Exercise to keep us supple
I hope you doing them wi a chuckle
In life all things they come and go
I hope this isna awfi slow
But go it will and we can cheer
We'll be together with all that's dear

Written by Ken Hutchison age 84

Echo Lizard

E is for easting which she loving
C is for climbing onto a thing
H is for hunting bugs which she can't do
O is for opal fruits which she is not aloud

L is for licks on the sofa
I is for insects which she loves
Z is for zzzz's while she sleeps a lot
A is for annoy in the mood she goes in with Mom
R is for reptile her class of animal
D is for looking like a Dino

Written by Hudson age 9

Hope in corona

I know corona is letting us down
I hope a cure is coming to town
I am grateful for my food
It puts me in a great mood
I am grateful for my Xbox
And my hot dogs
There's so much hope in this world
In every man woman and girl

Written by Hudson age 9

The Definition of Hope

Hope is the light that shines at the end of the tunnel, the
star the helps you find your way. It's the fire that keeps us
warm in coldest of days. Hope's light never falters.
Hope is the wind that lifts our hair and twists the leaves,
the snow that dances in the air before falling to our feet.
It's the rain that splashes the ground on the dry, hot days,
the sun that shines through the darkest of thunder clouds.
Hope is the pot of gold at the end of the rainbow.
Hope is the happiness of best friends laughing, the joy of
each new day. It's the wonder of trying something
different, the way curiosity pulls at us. Hope is the feeling
of the wishes in a well.
Hope is the Spring as it blooms with flowers
Hope always finds a way...

Written by Sophie age 11

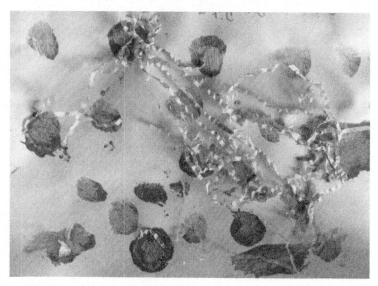

Created by Harry age 2

Places to go to for help and hope

Changes UK Addiction Services
0121 769 1000

St Basils
Help for young homeless people ages 16 -25
0121 772 2483

Samaritans
0330 094 5717

National Domestic Abuse Helpline
0808 2000 247
www.nationaldahelpline.org.uk/

The Men's Advice Line
For male domestic abuse survivors
0808 801 0327 (run by Respect)

The Mix
Free information and support for under 25s in the UK
0808 808 4994

National LGBT+ Domestic Abuse Helpline
0800 999 5428 (run by Galop)

We Are with You
Provide free and confidential support to people
experiencing issues with drugs, alcohol or mental health.
https://www.wearewithyou.org.uk/

Al-anon
Al-Anon provides support to anyone affected by someone else's drinking

Alcohol Concern
National agency on alcohol misuse

FRANK
Information, support and counselling for drug users and their families

rehab4addiction
A free helpline for those affected by substance misuse run by people who've beaten drug and alcohol rehab themselves

Domestic Abuse, Sexual Violence and Substance Use
Online service providing advise and support for substance use, domestic abuse and sexual violence

National Youth Advocacy Service
Information and advocacy service for children and young people up to 24 years.

Childnet
Childnet Hub is for young people aged 11-18, you'll find top tips, competitions, blogs and advice to help you to use the internet safely, responsibly and positively.

Action for Children
Support for vulnerable and neglected children and young people, and their families

Shelter
The UK's largest housing charity, gives information on housing rights, homelessness and state benefits.

Citizens' Advice Bureau (CAB)

Provides free, confidential and independent advice, including advice on housing. The website has information in Welsh, Bengali, Chinese, Gujarati, Punjabi and Urdu, as well as English, and allows you to locate your nearest CAB

www.citizensadvice.org.uk

Shelter (*Homelessness due to domestic violence*)

If you have to leave your home because of threats, abuse or intimidation, there may be safe places you can go to, such as refuges and temporary housing from the council. It may also be possible to stay in your home and make it safer.

Claiming homelessness

Under current law you can approach any Homeless Persons Unit if it is unsafe for you to remain in your home due to domestic violence. The Council is obliged to offer you temporary accommodation while they carry out their assessment or give you a decision on your application on the day. Housing law states that, 'It is not reasonable for a person to continue to occupy accommodation if it is probable that this will lead to domestic violence or other violence'. Violence means violence or threats of violence from another person, which are likely to be carried out.

Rethink

The largest severe mental illness charity in the UK

Mind

Information and support on mental health issues, including how to get help.

National Self Harm Network
A forum for survivors, professionals and family

Fast Forward
Information on drugs and alcohol education for youth.

Bursting the Bubble
Website for teenagers living with family violence.

Printed in Great Britain
by Amazon

62415567R00031